Original title:
Apple Blossom Dreams

Copyright © 2025 Creative Arts Management OÜ
All rights reserved.

Author: Liam Sterling
ISBN HARDBACK: 978-1-80586-340-3
ISBN PAPERBACK: 978-1-80586-812-5

Gazing at Petaled Horizons

In the orchard where laughter blooms,
Bumblebees dance in floral costumes.
A squirrel trips over a twig,
Swearing revenge on that sneaky big pig.

The sun glints off each tiny petal,
Drawing a map to the fruit that could settle.
But the only thing ripe is my silly grin,
As I wander 'round like a bee on gin.

Stories Written in Blossoms

Whispers of tales in the breeze,
A frog croaks love songs to the bees.
Each blossom displays its wild charm,
While ants march by, raising alarm.

One snail claims he'll win a race,
But falls asleep, dreaming of space.
Oh, petals giggle at this sight,
Comedy thrives in morning light!

Evening's Caress on Flowered Skin

The moon pranks the blossoms with glows,
While owls wear spectacles, striking poses.
Mice throw a party, cheese in hand,
While we laugh, not quite sure how we planned.

The shadows dance in a floral hall,
Where butterflies waltz, not caring at all.
It's a time when dreams play hide and seek,
In petals soft, my giggles peak.

Sunlight Draped in Petal Veils

Golden beams weave through sweet dew,
Tickling petals in a vibrant hue.
A ladybug struts, thinking she's grand,
While a grasshopper plays in a band.

Two daisies debate who's the fairest,
While their shadows grow long, the brightest.
Oh, life's a riot in garden dress,
Who knew petals could cause such a mess?

Serenity Draped in Floral Silks

In gardens where the critters play,
The bees wear hats and dance all day,
A squirrel juggles acorns with flair,
While flowers giggle, swaying with care.

A rabbit trots in a polka dot dress,
Claiming it's fashion, nothing but the best,
While daisies blush in shades of pink,
A sunflower winks, gives us a wink.

The breeze tickles petals so sweet,
While ladybugs tap dance with tiny feet,
The roses chat about the weather,
Sipping dew in a cozy tether.

Underneath this sky so blue,
Nature's comedy shines through,
With laughter echoing in the sun,
In floral silks, our joy's begun.

Hidden Visions Among the Branches

In a tree where squirrels play,
I saw a cat with shades today.
She danced on leaves, quite a sight,
Claiming she was queen of the night.

Bumblebees wearing tiny hats,
Held a tea party with the chitchatting cats.
Lemonade flowed from a bird's beak,
As they laughed and shared gossip, bold but meek.

Floral Imaginations Unfurled

A snail in boots tapped to the beat,
As flowers grooved on dainty feet.
Petals like confetti in the air,
They twirled and spun without a care.

A daffodil pondered, 'Where's my hat?'
While daisies giggled, soft and sprat.
They picked up pollen like a dance,
In this garden of fun, all took a chance.

Enchanted Meadows of Color

Caterpillars wearing capes, so grand,
Strolled through meadows, hand in hand.
They talked of dreams beneath the sun,
And plotted to race, just for fun.

A rainbow slipped and tumbled down,
Sold ice cream cones to the butterflies in town.
Laughter burst, like bubbles in spring,
In this quirky realm where the flowers sing.

Melodies in a Wind-Stirred Grove

Crickets played a jazzy tune,
While fireflies lit up the afternoon.
An orchestra of frogs joined the call,
As leaves swayed, inviting all.

A cheeky sparrow cracked a joke,
And nearby, a hedgehog broke into smoke.
In a symphony of chuckles and cheer,
Nature's band played, oh so dear.

Beneath the Fragrant Canopy

Beneath the branches, leaves do dance,
Buzzing bees give flowers a chance.
I tripped on roots, oh what a sight,
Laughter echoing, pure delight.

The sunbeams chuckle, warm and bright,
As squirrels play tag, a silly flight.
With every step, a giggle grows,
In this orchard, joy overflows.

Petal-Paved Pathways

Petals scatter like confetti falls,
A prankster breeze gives flowers their calls.
Chasing my hat, it twists and twirls,
A caper of colors, oh how it swirls!

My feet get tangled, I make a fuss,
In this garden of laughter, it's quite a plus.
A riddle in petals, a trail of glee,
Where smiles grow wild, and troubles flee.

Whispers from the Orchard's Lane

In the orchard's lane, the fruit jokes crack,
"Don't be sour!" they say, "Get back on track!"
A pear pokes fun at a shy little plum,
"Why so green? Come join the fun!"

Giggles erupt from under the trees,
As birds gossip softly in the warm breeze.
With every chuckle, the fruit starts to sway,
Hiding their laughter in a bright bouquet.

Enchanted Blooms at Dusk

As twilight beckons, shadows take flight,
The flowers whisper secrets of the night.
A daisy jokes, "I'm cooler than you!"
"I'm the star here," says the bloom that's blue.

Fireflies flicker, playing a game,
Lighting up giggles, never the same.
With every laugh, the night comes alive,
In this garden, joy will always thrive.

Moonlit Blooms and Silent Reflections

Under the moon, the flowers giggle,
Dancing shadows play, and they wiggle.
Stars above wink with a sly grin,
While petals dream of where they've been.

Whispers of bees, they plot and scheme,
Finding sweet nectar in a dream.
A butterfly lands, all dressed in style,
Winking at flowers with a charming smile.

Journey Through Blooming Pathways

On a cheerful path where daisies strut,
A squirrel in shades yells, 'Watch the nut!'
Rabbits in sneakers sprint on by,
While butterflies laugh and soar high.

Every step leads to a ticklish flower,
Who tells jokes at the top of the hour.
Petals giggle as the birds all sing,
Nature's laughter is a marvelous thing!

A Palette of Nature's Laughter

Colors explode like a merry parade,
Where giggles of blossoms in sunlight cascade.
The sun paints the ground in hues of delight,
While the wind whispers secrets in the light.

The grass tickles toes as folks walk near,
Blooming with joy—oops! Watch out for deer!
A grand bouquet plays hide and seek,
Leaving petals on boots, oh-so-cheek!

The Enchantment of the Season

In the season of giggles where blooms collide,
Each garden a stage for the joy inside.
Flowers wear hats, all crooked and bright,
Beneath sunny skies, everything feels right.

Chirping birds hold a concert for free,
As nature jests in wild harmony.
Laughter erupts from the trees up high,
Blooming tales that tickle the sky!

Whispers of Spring's Serenade

In a garden where no one cares,
Laughter floats through fragrant airs.
Bees wear hats; the butterflies dance,
A squirrel rolls by in a silly prance.

Sunshine chases clouds away,
While the rabbits plot a prank today.
The flowers gossip, petals sway,
About the mushrooms gone astray.

Petals in the Breeze

Petals flutter like they're lost,
Chasing each other, what a cost!
One lands on a snoring cat,
He wakes up mad, "What was that?"

A picnic's set, with ants in line,
Stealing crumbs, oh so fine!
But when they trip, it's quite the scene,
A conga line gone very green.

Orchard's Gentle Reverie

Silly squirrels, they take their bets,
Who can climb the tree with the best sets.
They argue, laugh, and then they fall,
Landing in baskets; oh, what a haul!

The sun sets slow, the day is done,
The fruit bats venture out for fun.
Chasing starbugs in the night,
Making mischief till the light.

Secrets Beneath the Bloom

Under blooms, a secret crew,
Rabbits whisper plans anew.
They plot to swindle a farmer's pie,
With clever tricks as they rush by.

A dandelion's got a crush,
On a ladybug in a rush.
They twirl and spin without a care,
In a whirlwind of bright spring air.

Beneath the Fragile Canopy

Beneath the branches, bees play tag,
Hiding from squirrels that wiggle and brag.
Petals are giggling, dancing in tune,
While rabbits do hop, twirling like a balloon.

A ladybug slips, does a comic fall,
Chuckling leaves hear, they can't help but call.
Sunshine spills laughter over the grass,
As butterflies bicker, 'Who's first in class?'

A Symphony of Nature's Colors

Colors collide in a silly parade,
Where daisies wear shades, looking quite staid.
Dandelions chuckle, 'We're more than a weed!'
While clovers play cards, the odd little breed.

The robin sings high, but the worm rolls its eyes,
'Not again!' it exclaims, 'Oh, what a surprise!'
Harmony's chaos in nature's bright play,
As rain makes a splash, laughing all the way.

Fluttering Dreams on Branches

Journal of leaves holds whispers of dreams,
Gossiping birds craft fanciful themes.
Squirrels debate, what's the best acorn?
While foxes roll over like they're just reborn.

Twists of the breeze tickle the tree,
It giggles delight, 'Oh, be light and free!'
A dance on the wind, a hop in the air,
Each moment a joke, a whimsical flare.

The Art of Pollination's Kiss

Bees wear tuxedos, looking quite sly,
Mastering dances, buzzing on by.
Flowers all wink with colorful glee,
'Come join the ball!' they call to the bee.

The fragrance of trouble, sweet pollen so bright,
Turns butterflies dizzy, a fluttering flight.
In joyous rebellion, nature does play,
With laughter and mischief brightening the day.

Delicate Dreams on Soft Wings

Tiny wings flutter by,
Wearing dew as a cape,
Chasing crumbs through the sky,
In this garden escape.

Ladybugs dance round and round,
On petals soft as cream,
Whispers of laughter abound,
In this silly dream.

Bumblebees sing off-key,
With tunes made of honey,
They sip with such glee,
Life's sweet and so funny.

Rain drops can't stop the fun,
As puddles become ponds,
Splashing under the sun,
Where magic responds.

The Serenity of Unfurling

Petals stretch with a yawn,
Morning light tickles,
Caressing them till dawn,
With cheeky little giggles.

Buds burst like popcorn pops,
In a riot of cheer,
Blossoms dance and swap,
Their colors so dear.

Fluffy clouds float on air,
Tickling the trees' tops,
Nature's funny affair,
Where hilarity never stops.

A snail takes a grand leap,
Into mud with a wiggle,
In this joy, we can seep,
And join in the wiggle.

Portrait of a Petal Dreamer

A flower wears a hat,
Made of sunshine's best,
Admiring all that,
In a polka dot vest.

Bees with tiny sunglasses,
Practicing their style,
Pollinating with pizzazz,
Making every flower smile.

A wandering breeze jokes,
Tickling each petal's face,
While swirling funny blokes,
In a fragrant embrace.

Life's a vibrant swirl,
Where laughter takes flight,
In this floral whirl,
Everything feels just right.

Dreams in the Glow of Spring

Springtime's here with a wink,
As crocuses start to dance,
Flowers playfully link,
In a fragrant romance.

Daffodils wear big grins,
As the daisies all cheer,
Each petal spins and spins,
With joy that feels so near.

Chirping frogs sing their views,
In this garden delight,
With silly little blues,
Making day turn to night.

A breeze brings giggles in tow,
As leaves flutter high,
Together they'll grow,
Under a silly sky.

Garden of Ephemeral Fantasies

In the garden, bees wear hats,
Chasing flowers in silly spats.
Daisies giggle, tulips cheer,
While squirrels juggle nuts, oh dear!

Frogs in ties jump with flair,
Singing tunes without a care.
Butterflies in polka dots,
Dance around the nearby pots.

Portraits of a Shimmering Season

Suited pigeons strut in lines,
Chasing shadows, sipping wines.
Ladybugs sip on iced tea,
While ants show off their new marquee.

Dandelions wear crowns of gold,
Revealing secrets never told.
With every gust, a sneeze anew,
Of pollen dreams that drift askew.

Whispers of Spring's Awakening

The sun peeks through with a grin,
Teasing tulips, let the fun begin!
Worms in top hats twist and twirl,
While spiders weave a dance, oh pearl!

Chirpy birds hum a cheeky song,
As wind does cartwheels all along.
Grasshoppers leap in hula hoops,
While clouds join in of fluffy groups.

Petals' Sway in Gentle Breezes

Petals waltz in breezy bliss,
As bees parade with a little twist.
Hummingbirds play hide-and-seek,
While daisies giggle, "Look, unique!"

A snail dons shades, looking chic,
With every shell, a new critique.
Rain drops laugh, then give a cheer,
Spring's sweet folly, loud and clear!

Whirlwind of Petal Dreams

In a twirl of twigs and petals,
Squirrels dance with bouncing kettles.
Bees wear hats and ride on toys,
While rabbits play with joyful noise.

Chasing clouds with silly grins,
The flowers giggle, sharing wins.
A breeze whispers a secret joke,
While butterflies take tiny pokes.

In the chaos, laughter springs,
As mischief blooms on feathered wings.
Each tree sways in playful glee,
The sky bursts forth with jubilee.

In this dreamscape, wild and bright,
Frolicking critters take to flight.
A whirlwind spins, dreams take stride,
In a land where fun won't hide.

Soft Hues of an Orchard Reverie

In orchards where the colors blend,
Chickens cluck and make new trends.
They don their hats, all frilly bright,
As ducks perform a comical flight.

The sun winks down on clever rows,
While laughing veggies strike a pose.
A carrot whispers with a grin,
"Here comes the rabble, let's take a spin!"

The trees blush pink in morning light,
While furry critters start their fight.
The pears debate who's round and nice,
While apricots roll like a dice.

In soft hues, mischief spins wide,
Laughter echoes, joy can't hide.
In corners where the berries dream,
A fruity carnival, it would seem.

The Language of Fluttering Leaves

Leaves chatter in a silly dance,
They gossip, giggle and take a chance.
"Who wore it best?" they leafily say,
As breezes toss them in wild play.

A nutty squirrel joins the crew,
He tells a tale that's slightly askew.
"Did you hear the rumor on the vine,
That strawberries can't compose a line?"

With rustling skirts, the branches splay,
They laugh and sway away the day.
A rumor spreads, "The sky's a clown!"
As leisurely clouds drift up and down.

Like whispers shared between best pals,
They prance around the funny gales.
In the chatter of the leafy trees,
Is a world of laughter caught in the breeze.

Dreams Cradled in Pink

In pink embrace, all dreams take flight,
Pigs in tutus twirl in delight.
A clumsy bear trips on a vine,
As cherries giggle, sipping wine.

The kittens dance on fluffy trees,
As clouds roll in with silly ease.
A ticklish breeze begins to play,
As iambic ants march on their way.

With sprightly steps, the orchard sings,
Of pudding pies and butterfly flings.
Each blossom winks with cheeky flair,
As dreams unfold without a care.

In dreamy hues of laughter bright,
Joy rides on the wings of light.
Cradled gently in hues of fun,
The orchard's laughter has just begun.

Chasing Shadows in the Vineyards

In the vineyard, shadows sway,
Grapes giggle and roll away.
A squirrel slipped, oh what a sight,
Chased by laughter, what a fright!

Underneath the leafy vines,
A rabbit plays, it draws some lines.
The sun in jest is shining bright,
Making shadows dance with delight.

Bottles pop with fizzy cheer,
As friends unite to sing and cheer.
But watch your step for grape juice spills,
You might just slip and get your thrills!

With every laugh and playful glance,
The vineyard blooms, it starts to prance.
Let's chase the shadows, have some fun,
The day is bright, the race's begun!

Wishes Carried by the Breeze

A kite above begins to glide,
With wishes whispered, hearts open wide.
The wind laughs, it knows our dreams,
It tickles cheeks and bursts at seams.

Dance in fields where daisies sway,
Each step we take leads us astray.
A tumble here, a giggle there,
The breeze becomes a playful dare.

Through meadows bright, we skip and spin,
Chasing laughter, let joy begin.
But hold your hats, the gust is keen,
It steals a pie—oh what a scene!

With every wish upon the breeze,
We catch the laughter, feel the ease.
So let's delight in all we see,
As summer's fun sets our hearts free!

Heartbeats of Midspring

In springtime's dance, the flowers leap,
While bees do buzz and dreams we keep.
A puppy sniffs and chases tails,
As butterflies weave funny trails.

Grass tickles toes, a playful shout,
As kids race by, there's no doubt.
A picnic spread, the ants invade,
They'll steal your snacks, oh that brigade!

The sunshine beams with silly rays,
Creating shadows that hop and play.
We laugh so hard, we start to cry,
As birds join in, their tunes awry.

Heartbeats quicken with each laugh,
We find the spice in nature's path.
With springtime's joy, our spirits rise,
As we embrace this sweet surprise!

The Garden's Secrets Unveiled

In the garden, secrets cheer,
Snapdragons sneer, they're hiding near.
A gnome with a hat, a sly little grin,
Whispers jokes as we sit in spin.

Carrots plot their great escape,
While tomatoes hide in leafy drape.
Cucumbers roll, playing hide and seek,
Chasing giggles, that's their peak!

A bee puts on a dapper show,
With flowered bowtie, oh what a pro!
As worms tell tales beneath the ground,
The garden bursts with laughter sound.

With every bloom, a twisty prank,
Nature chuckles down by the bank.
Our secret garden, wild and free,
Is full of laughter—come see with me!

The Fragrance of Tomorrow

In the orchard, we dance with delight,
Sipping honey from flowers, oh what a sight.
The bees wear sunglasses, quite the display,
Buzzing to tunes as they sip all day.

An old crow jokes, 'You've got no chance,'
While we twirl around in a silly glance.
With petals as hats, we prance around,
Laughing as gravity pulls us to the ground.

Beneath the Canopy of Pink

Underneath branches, our giggles erupt,
We tickle the bumblebees, oh how they disrupt!
The ground covered in blush, what a sight to see,
Spreading laughter like seeds, wild and free.

A squirrel in a bowtie, so dapper, so spry,
Critiques our moves, saying, 'Why even try?'
But a cartwheel later, he's taken aback,
Rolling in petals, now he's joined the pack.

Nectar of Transient Moments

We gather sweet nectar; it's sticky but fun,
Pigeon coin toss, is he a bird or a bun?
With dresses of petals and crowns made of leaves,
We prank every cloud, saying, 'Who even grieves?'

The sun peeks shyly, holding back its blush,
While we make a whirlpool, waiting for the hush.
A ladybug joins with a wink and a spin,
In a whirl of bright laughter, we tuck our chins.

Stars Lost in Orchard Shadows

Stars twinkle playfully, peeking from trees,
While we glide through shadows, as light as a breeze.
An owl shouts, 'Quiet! There's no need to yell!'
But we've turned the orchard into our own festival.

The moon rakes leaves, making us giggle,
As we hide from the giggles, in fits we wiggle.
With dreams in our pockets and laughter to share,
We dance under starlight, without a single care.

The Dance of Fragile Petals

In a breeze, they swirl and twirl,
Catching giggles, in their whirl.
Bumblebees join in the fun,
They dance till day is done.

With polka dots and tiny wings,
They sip nectar, oh, the flings!
Petals blush in golden light,
Turning daydreams into flight.

Underneath the maple tree,
They share tales of jubilee.
Grasshoppers leap with such delight,
In this garden, all feels right.

So come and join this merry spree,
With petals swirling, wild and free.
A fairy tale, let's all resolve,
In this dance, we all evolve.

Blossoms Beneath the Silver Moon

Under moonbeams, whispers rise,
Petals giggle, to our surprise.
Crickets play a heady tune,
As flowers sway beneath the moon.

A raccoon dons a flowery hat,
Dances with an old, wise cat.
Fireflies twinkle, spark and glide,
Join in all this moonlit pride.

Pollen sprinkles like confetti,
While frogs croak, oh-so-setty.
Laughter echoes through the night,
As blossoms bloom in sheer delight.

If you listen close, you'll hear,
The floral giggles drawing near.
In this garden, pure and bright,
Beneath the silver moonlight.

Echoes of Floral Lullabies

In the garden, whispers hum,
With melodies that make you numb.
Petals sharing silly rhymes,
Giggling through the passing times.

Little ladybugs in rows,
Wearing hats made of rose.
Chasing dreams on tiny wings,
While the whole garden sings.

Dewdrops pop like bubblegum,
Frogs croon softly, oh-so-come!
Each flower sways, with gentle grace,
In this sweet, enchanted place.

Let's hold hands and sway along,
With flowers, we will sing a song.
Echoes sweet of laughter sigh,
Drifting softly, oh, how we fly.

Garden's Rhapsody in Bloom

A rhapsody of colors bright,
In the garden, pure delight.
Bees wear ties, so dapper and neat,
While blossoms sway, dancing to the beat.

Buttercups giggle in the sun,
Throwing parties, oh what fun!
Ferns play cards, so sly and bold,
Telling tales of days of old.

Sunflowers wave, strutting tall,
Wishing everyone would call.
A singing daisy takes the lead,
With every petal, plant a seed.

In this rhapsody, hearts will bloom,
Filling the air with sweet perfume.
Join the fun, let laughter ring,
In this garden, life's a fling.

Cradled in Floral Embrace

In the garden, bees do dance,
Tickling petals, oh, what a chance!
A sneaky squirrel with a playful grin,
Swipes a bloom, and chaos begins!

Worms wear hats, it's quite absurd,
While frogs in bowties croak a word.
A dandelion puffs, like fluffy cheese,
And giggles burst upon the breeze!

A snail in shades, oh what a sight,
Glides through grass, slow as night.
Ladybugs with tiny wheels,
Race for treats, and squeal their squeals!

Sunshine spills, a golden dance,
Every flower gets a chance.
In this funny, floral range,
Laughter blooms in every strange.

Colorful Daydreams of Spring

Tulips wear their vibrant hats,
As butterflies flirt with the chittering gnats.
A daisy trips, falls on its face,
While a grumpy toad claims his space!

The tulip's gossip, oh so loud,
Makes the bees feel quite so proud.
Tiny ants march, a soldier brigade,
Stealing crumbs, they rarely fade.

Crickets sing a silly tune,
While blooms sway like dancing loons.
Nothing's perfect; that's the key,
In springtime's laugh, it's all so free!

Colors clash, a joyful fight,
Roses blush in pure delight.
With petals caught in playful schemes,
Life's a jest in springtime dreams.

Whispers Among the Blossoms

Bumblebees chat in secret codes,
While daisies play leapfrog on the roads.
A dandelion wishes to be a star,
But grabs a bee, and they don't go far.

Pollen parties, a wild affair,
Blooming friends without a care.
Lilies laugh at how they sway,
Finding joy in every play!

A flower sneezes, sends seeds flying,
While chubby caterpillars, oh so trying,
Slip and slide on petals wide,
As blooming laughter cannot hide.

Whispers of the wind do spin,
In this garden of cheeky kin.
With every rustle, a giggle bursts,
Nature's humor, always first!

Touched by Nature's Brush

The artist's hand paints the scene,
With splashes of colors bright and keen.
A butterfly's twirl, a clumsy flight,
Stirs up giggles, pure delight!

The daisies sway, bowing low,
While tulips gossip, putting on a show.
A bumblebee gets stuck in glee,
In circles round, like a jigged-up spree!

Violets in hats, a fashion craze,
Pose for selfies in the sun's warm rays.
A bunny hops with a chuckling sound,
While petals tumble all around.

The sky bursts golden, with laughter loud,
As flowers party, feeling proud.
In this scene, where silliness dwells,
'Tis nature's magic, as everyone tells!

Canvas of Petal-Laden Skies

Beneath a tree, I cast my gaze,
Petals drifting in a playful haze.
A bee buzzed by in college style,
Wearing shades, it danced a while.

Each flower giggled as it swayed,
In clumps of color, a jester's parade.
I tip my hat to the branch so bold,
It swats the wasp, like stories of old.

What trickery lies within this bloom?
A garden dance, or the start of a zoom?
I tossed a seed; it rolled like a dream,
And sprouted a vine with a quirky theme.

Nature's laughter, a vibrant play,
As petals twirl in mad ballet.
With every giggle, the world spins bright,
In the canvas of spring, all feels just right.

Vows of the Orchard's Heart

In a grove where whispers play,
A squirrel proposed in a nutty way.
Underneath the branches we laughed out loud,
While birds all cheered, a feathered crowd.

"I'll give you acorns," the squirrel swore,
"Stick by me, and you'll never be bored!"
With rings of twigs, the vows were set,
A union forged, no chance of regret.

As blooms erupted with colors grand,
I wondered if they had a plan so planned.
"Will there be cake in your world so bright?"
"Only if we sprinkle it with mud pie slights!"

So they danced, the leaves did cheer,
In a wedding where nothing was clear.
With wild abandon, love took its stance,
In the orchard's heart, they wobbled their dance.

The Grapevine's Gentle Murmur

Amidst the vines, I heard a chit,
Grapes were gossiping, oh what a bit!
"They say the pears are having a ball,
Dancing with plums, they're quite the thrall!"

"Who needs champagne when you've got juice?
We'll just rollick, let loose, let loose!"
The leaves all giggled, a gentle sway,
In the vineyard's jive, they laughed away.

The shadows flickered, the sun hid its beams,
Whispers wandered in whimsical dreams.
As fruits exchanged tales over sweet and sour,
I clutched a berry, expecting a power.

But wait! A critter with shoes so bright,
Joined in the fray on this magical night.
With every plop and every croon,
The vines twined tighter like a cheeky tune.

Awakening Wonder

In morning mist, I found a grin,
A ladybug danced, her head in a spin.
She sipped the dew while wiggling her toes,
In a twirling fate that nobody knows.

The flowers stretched, yawning aloud,
As the sun peeked in, creating a crowd.
With petals swirling in an airy shout,
The whole garden giggled; there was no doubt.

"Who will lead today's playful race?"
The daisies dared with a friendly trace.
So off they went, in a blooming spree,
Chasing the bumblebees, clever and free.

A napkin blew across the grass,
"Oh look!" said the rose, "Here comes the sass!"
And so they played till twilight's gleam,
In a world filled with magic, like a vibrant dream.

Serenade of Budding Colors

In the garden, bees do dance,
Chasing petals, taking a chance.
Every bloom wears a silly hat,
As the wind plays with the chatting cat.

Butterflies wear shoes of gold,
Strutting around, being bold.
Laughter bubbles like a bright brook,
Nature's jesters on a playful nook.

A squirrel sings to his grandpa tree,
Recounting tales of raucous glee.
Colors swirl in a grand ballet,
As the sun joins in to play.

Clouds drift by, some snicker and tease,
With jokes that tickle the buzzing bees.
Each bloom has giggles up their sleeves,
In this riot of colors, fun weaves.

A Canvas of Soft Petal Hues

Here lies a painter with a pout,
Stirring petals, there's no doubt.
Splashes of pink on a grassy sheet,
Giggles echo with each brush's beat.

A rogue sunbeam steals the show,
As daisies wink, flirting with snow.
While daffodils snicker all day long,
We're in a world where all feel strong.

Funny faces on each green stem,
Sharing whispers like a secret gem.
Together they frolic, donning a crown,
In this colorful stage where no one's down.

A rainbow prances, full of zest,
With every color trying its best.
The painter chuckles, brushes in tow,
Creating joy where the petals grow.

The Sweetness of Morning Dew

Morning's dew drops laugh and play,
Tickling flowers at the break of day.
Every blade wears a glistening hat,
As squirrels pause, feeling quite fat.

Crickets hum a cheeky tune,
Under the watch of a sleepy moon.
A ladybug joins the sprightly crew,
Sneaking snacks, feeling brand new.

Frogs croak jokes, a ribbit or two,
While tulips sway, saying 'who knew?'
The grass beams bright, dousing the sun,
In this playful realm, we all have fun.

Caterpillars snag a quick dance,
Turning leaves into a sprightly chance.
In the air, mischief brews anew,
With sweet giggles of morning dew.

In the Orchard of Dreams

In the orchard, whispers bounce around,
Fruit trees chuckle on solid ground.
With every breeze, they shake and sway,
As the wind teases them to play.

Cherries blush while pears sing loud,
A watermelon wearing a leafy shroud.
Under crates, old apples boast,
Telling tales of when they were most.

Grasshoppers share a joke or three,
While a hedgehog rolls with glee.
The soil grins beneath our feet,
In this joyous orchard, life is sweet.

Roll out the barrels, let laughter ring,
Nature's chorus is here to sing.
In this vibrant place, spirits gleam,
Filled with happiness, what a dream!

In the Shade of Blooming Wonder

Underneath a tree so grand,
I found a hat, not quite my brand.
A squirrel wore it with such flair,
I laughed so hard, I lost my hair.

The petals fell like snow, so light,
Dancing softly in my sight.
A bee joined in the silly waltz,
I asked it why—no word, just vaults.

The grass tickled my toes just right,
While birds serenaded with delight.
A worm joined in, so full of glee,
He moonwalked past, quite daredevil-y.

With laughter ringing in the air,
I chased a breeze without a care.
The world felt like a joyful scheme,
In the shade of blooming, wild dreams.

Chasing the Softest Petals

I chased a petal that took flight,
It floated down to my delight.
A puppy pounced, so full of cheer,
We both fell down in giggles, dear.

The flowers whispered jokes so sly,
While butterflies posed, oh my, oh my!
I tried to catch one in my hand,
But slipped and landed in the sand.

Soon bees joined in on this fine game,
They buzzed and spun, but felt no shame.
The petals laughed, they had a blast,
While I just rolled in grass so fast.

A ladybug said, "What's the fuss?"
I shrugged and laughed, felt quite the plus.
In the chase of joy and sunny sparks,
Each petal danced, leaving happy marks.

Threads of Springtime's Tapestry

In this quirky quilt of hue,
I stitched a patch of socks, it's true!
With scattered threads and colors bright,
I snagged a bird, oh what a sight!

The daisies cheered on every stitch,
While sunbeams danced, they did a glitch.
My cat wore a flower crown so neat,
She strutted like a little diva treat.

A woven dream with laughs in store,
I added a patch of humor more.
With giggles threaded in between,
This tapestry turned quite the scene.

As petals joined the fabric's play,
I found a rose who had something to say.
Each thread a giggle, every hue a laugh,
In spring's fine quilt, our joyful craft.

Scent of the Unspoken Promise

A whiff of spring, so fresh and bright,
It tickled my nose, what a delight!
I sneezed so loud, the birds took flight,
They chirped and laughed, what a silly sight.

From blooms above, a fragrance swirled,
A dance of scents in laughter twirled.
Each flower blushed with rosy pride,
While bees buzzed about, joy as their guide.

A gopher popped up with a grin,
Said, "This aroma sure gets me in!"
I offered him a petal treat,
We both giggled, life was sweet.

With scents of joy in every breeze,
We spun around with such great ease.
The promise hung like perfume's glow,
In this fun garden, love did grow.

Petal-Gilded Dreams

In a garden where giggles grow,
A bee wears sunglasses, don't you know?
The daisies dance, they trip and fall,
While butterflies play catch, oh what a ball!

A snail races slow, with style so grand,
He's got a tiny top hat, isn't it planned?
The flowers giggle, they're in the zone,
Playing hopscotch on the garden stone!

The sun winks down with a cheeky flair,
Tickling the petals, do they even care?
A grasshopper sings, can't hit a note,
While ants march by in a tiny boat!

So here in this world where whimsy thrives,
Nature chuckles, and laughter arrives.
Join the parade of petals, it seems,
In this frolicsome realm of gilded dreams.

Garden of Forgotten Wishes

In a place where wishes go to hide,
A frog plays chess with a snail, so spry.
The moonlight giggles over growing vines,
As flowers whisper silly punchlines.

Old gnomes reminisce over cups of tea,
Swapping tall tales beneath the cedar tree.
A worm's got jokes, or so he says,
While the daisies chuckle in the sun's rays.

The breeze tells secrets of long-lost dreams,
As butterflies burst out in giggly screams.
Petunias gossip about the latest buzz,
While bees hold court, 'cause that's just because!

So stroll through this garden where laughter grows,
With flora and fauna that everyone knows.
In this haven of wishes, let joy take flight,
With whimsical whispers all through the night.

Enigma of the Floral Dawn

When morning breaks in colors so bright,
The sun wakes up, it's quite a sight!
A flower yawns, throws a petal or two,
While a squirrel steals breakfast—how rude, who knew?

The daisies conspire, a plot to tease,
Laughing at robins who trip on the breeze.
A toad croaks loudly, the punchline is done,
As the tulips all giggle—oh, wasn't that fun?

Sunbeams paint the laughter on every leaf,
While butterflies flutter, it's a comic relief.
The early dew glistens like tiny bling,
In this floral realm where the choirs sing!

So join in the fun at the break of day,
Where flowers laugh in their own special way.
The enigma unfolds, with smiles abound,
In the mischievous glow of the floral dawn.

Reverence for Nature's Magic

In a world where the oddities play,
A parrot tells stories in a snazzy way.
The trees clap their hands in delightful cheer,
As squirrels perform, with a laugh and a leer.

Petals burst forth with a giggle and sway,
Unicorns prance, giving rainbows their play.
A raccoon wears glasses, reading a book,
While flowers gather 'round for a heartfelt look.

The moon spills giggles like glittering streams,
As the night blooms magic, fulfilling wild dreams.
With fireflies blinking in mischief they gleam,
Dancing to the tune of a whispered scheme.

So cherish this revelry, wild and bright,
Where nature's humor brings wondrous delight.
In reverence we gather, our hearts in a mirth,
For the joy of the magic that dwells on this earth.

Transience in Fragrance

In a garden where blunders bloom,
Bees buzz loudly, plotting their doom.
Petals flutter, drinks served by bees,
Sipping nectar, with utmost ease.

A squirrel sneezes in dainty surprise,
As flowers giggle, rolling their eyes.
The pollen floats like confetti in air,
While butterflies pose without a care.

Morning dew plays hide and seek,
With sunshine peeking, they both sneak.
And in the chaos, the ants march dense,
Claiming their ground, with little suspense.

Yet as the sun sets, night's cloak begins,
The flowers fold up, losing their grins.
In this waltz of life, ever so sweet,
Who knew a garden could be so neat?

A Dance of Delicate Hues

Colors twirl in a merry spree,
Petals prancing, as bright as can be.
Tulips waltz, and daisies spin,
With ladybugs watching, no need to grin.

A robins' tune starts the afternoon,
While dancing blooms hum a funny tune.
They argue on which shade rules the day,
Which flower's flair leads the ballet.

A rogue wind sweeps, petals take flight,
Sailing away, out of sheer delight.
Dancing partners in mischief embrace,
As bees get dizzy in the race.

Yet as twilight creeps in to claim,
Colors fade, and they're never the same.
With laughter lingering in the breeze,
All bow down, till night's calm, they seize.

Echoes of Floral Wishes

Whispers of petals, dreams take a leap,
Wishing on pollen, in silence they peep.
A dandelion shouts, 'Make a wish quick!'
But alas! A breeze makes it vanish, oh trick!

Lily chuckles, 'I'm quite the show!'
While sunflowers giggle, putting on glow.
A shy rose blushes at the funny parade,
Joining the laughter with thoughts unafraid.

In the chaos, a gnome stumbles tall,
Tripping on roots, but still stands small.
He mumbles wishes with a fumble and twist,
While flowers cheer for the magic they missed.

As night falls softly with stars in view,
The wishes linger, cozy and true.
With laughter echoing in moon's silver light,
Floral dreams dance, till the end of the night.

Morning Dew on Silken Leaves

Glistening dew drops like tiny bold balls,
Trickling down leaves, giggling in thralls.
A leaf makes whispers, with rustles of cheer,
Inviting a snail for a morning beer.

Sunlight bursts forth, chasing shadows away,
Sprinkling laughter on this bright day.
A dandy little bug, with spectacles grand,
Laments the morning needs a dance band.

They boogie and sway, on this vibrant quilt,
While raindrops tease in their chilly spilt.
The laughter imprints on each petal's face,
As nature's own choir sings in their place.

And with the sunset, the leaves whisper low,
'What a silly day, now take it slow!'
As dreams take flight, in the twilight's embrace,
Morning dew smiles, leaving not a trace.

Reflections in Petal Waters

A squirrel in shades, all dressed up fine,
Chasing his tail, with a comical line.
Petals drift down like confetti bright,
He slips on a blush—what a silly sight!

The bees in a frenzy, they dance and buzz,
Trying to impress the flowers because.
They wear tiny hats made of dewdrop cheer,
Winging their way, buzzing loud for clear!

A ladybug winks, she's the queen tonight,
Strutting her spots in the soft moonlight.
With laughter unbridled, the garden hums,
As nature giggles, and joyfully drums.

The pond holds reflections of all things bright,
A crow takes a dip—what a silly fright!
And we all watch, with laughter that streams,
In this garden realm of funny dreams.

A Pilgrimage to Floral Serenity

Two worms in a race, they wiggle and squirm,
Arguing over who'll eat the best fern.
With a pause for a snack, they munch and they chew,
Saying, "This leaf tastes just like honeydew!"

The tulips gossip in colorful dress,
"Last year's bee buzz was a total mess!"
They swap silly tales with a petal swirl,
"Did you hear 'bout the snail? She danced a whirl!"

A group of tall daisies, with stems so proud,
Attempting a wave to a passing cloud.
Instead, they wobble and sway with a laugh,
"Oh dear, who knew we'd become a giraffe!"

Their laughter erupts, a pollen spree,
As the breeze carries secrets, wild and free.
They celebrate spring with their whimsical ways,
In a garden alive, where happiness plays.

Harmony in Bloom's Embrace

An awkward little frog leaps with a cheer,
Singing to bees, so they'll all gather near.
But he slips on a petal and makes quite a splash,
Landing with style—what a glorious crash!

The butterflies flutter, in tutus they play,
Joining the frog in his humorous way.
One twists and twirls, in a floral fade,
"Look at me, look at me! I'm a colorful braid!"

A hedgehog rolls by, in shades of bright green,
Critiquing the flowers, "You don't look serene!"
With laughter, the daisies bloom wide and grand,
"Join us, dear hedgehog, in our merry band!"

In this scene of joy, as the petals kiss air,
Nature's own jesters sprinkle fun everywhere.
With each little giggle, the flowers all sway,
In the harmony found in this whimsical play.

Kaleidoscope of Springtime Blooms

The tulips are twerking, with laughs on the breeze,
The sunflowers chuckle, "Can you match our ease?"
A bumblebee tumbles in vibrant delight,
Bellyflopping blooms in a colorful flight!

The daisies have issues with fashion and flair,
Complaining of petals that crunch when they wear.
"Last spring's designs were a total disgrace,
Now everyone's stinging with floral embrace!"

A cunning chipmunk with pockets of seeds,
Shares wacky tales of his hilarious deeds.
"Watch me!" he shouts, as he leaps for a nut,
But he trips in a daisy, landing with a thud!

The garden erupts with a cheerful, loud roar,
Nature's own laughter, a grand encore.
In this kaleidoscope of colors and laughs,
Spring's merry jesters with big, silly chafs!

Blossoms of a Wistful Heart

In a garden filled with giggles,
Petals dance like happy sprinkles,
Bumblebees in tiny hats,
Wobbling 'round like silly rats.

The sunbeam wears a bright blue tie,
As we chase clouds that drift and fly,
Every bloom throws a cheeky wink,
While squirrels plot and smile, I think.

Laughter bubbles in the breeze,
Tickling flowers, oh how they tease,
With pollen pockets and a grin,
A race against the squirrels begins.

Here in this land of floral cheer,
I swear I heard a flower leer,
As petals giggle, bloom and sway,
My heart just skips at play today.

Vibrant Echoes in Floral Whispers

In fields where flowers prance and tease,
The daisies play, they aim to please,
Sunsets dance with pastel spark,
While all around, there's laughter's lark.

A tulip trips, a daffodil slips,
Whispering secrets in floral quips,
The pinks and yellows start to brawl,
In a silly, fragrant free-for-all.

Bees don tuxedos, oh what a sight!
Planning a ball, it feels just right,
While butterflies laugh at their prissy ways,
Reacting to pollen like kids who play.

Each bloom holds stories of whimsy and cheer,
With every rustle, I lean in to hear,
Their giggles and whispers blend in the air,
A carnival of petals, so joyful and rare.

Ethereal Lullabies of Spring

In a garden where dreams take flight,
The petals sing through day and night,
Ladybugs sport their dapper hats,
As grasshoppers dance with silly spats.

A breeze steals whispers from flower to tree,
Poking fun at the puppy's glee,
With trunks that giggle and branches that sway,
Nature's own joke in a breezy ballet.

Frogs croak rhythms, a comical tune,
As crickets join with a swoon and a swoon,
Each bloom releases a merry sigh,
While dreaming of cakes in the sky up high.

Oh, what a laughter-filled serenade,
Creating memories that never fade,
With petals fluttering, life takes a leap,
In springtime's magic, we laugh and we peep.

Petal-Capped Memories

With petals piled high on heads like crowns,
We prance and skip, no reason for frowns,
A dandelion's wishes float by in gleeful jest,
While giggles spill out from hearts, feeling blessed.

The tulips organize a dance-off grand,
While daisies cheer from their patch of land,
Oh, the buzzing bees act like tiny DJs,
Spinning sweet tunes to our tangled ballet.

Chasing butterflies with silly goals,
Like racecars running on flowered strolls,
Their wings fluttering, bright as the sun,
It's a game of laughter, let's have some fun!

As petals fall soft like whispers of glee,
I hold all these moments, oh can't you see?
In this garden of dreams, with laughs to behold,
Petal-capped memories forever unfold.

After the Storm

Raindrops dance on leaves so green,
A soggy hat upon my bean.
The winds howl like a hungry cat,
Yet here I stand, a soggy brat.

Puddles form a tiny sea,
Splashing laughter, oh so free.
I leap and jump, a giddy flop,
As rainbows peek, we all just stop.

Blossoms Speak

Whispering petals in the breeze,
Sharing secrets with the bees.
They giggle softly, 'Can you see?'
A dancing sprout, just like me!

'Why do you frown, oh grumpy flower?'
One bud chirps from its leafy tower.
'Life's a pop quiz, but why fret?
It's just a joke we won't forget!'

Nature's Pink Confessions

Buds in pink are up to tricks,
Making up stories, oh what a mix!
'I'm a fairy, wild and free!'
Squeaks a petal, a laughter spree.

Lilies giggle in vibrant hues,
As daisies try on silly shoes.
'What's a flower without some flair?'
They prance about without a care!

Verses from the Fruitful Realm

Fruits are chatting, oh what a tease,
Bananas swing from the leafy trees.
'Tell a joke!' cries out a plum,
While apples giggle—'Oh, here we come!'

Cherries chuckle, 'We're so divine!'
A rascal grape shouts, 'Pass the wine!'
In this realm, laughter's the game,
Juicy tales, never the same.

Garden of Whimsical Sighs

In a garden where dreams take flight,
Twirling daisies, oh what a sight!
'Tickle me pink!' the roses cry,
As butterflies drift just nearby.

A gnome sneezes—'Choo! Excuse me!'
The flowers laugh with jubilee.
Mirthful whispers fill the air,
In this garden, joy's everywhere!

Breath of Petals in Dusk

In the twilight's gentle sway,
Flowers giggle, night at play.
Bees are buzzing in a race,
Dancing all without a trace.

Crickets chirp a silly tune,
To the light of the silver moon.
Petals whisper, secrets bright,
Tickling shadows, out of sight.

Dew drops laugh upon the leaves,
While the sleepy garden heaves.
Clouds drift by with silly faces,
In this world of dreamy places.

As night falls, the blooms conspire,
To share jokes like a wild choir.
With a wink, they all unite,
In the crazy, starry night.

Ode to Days of Blooming Glory

Oh, the colors, vivid, bold,
The secrets that they lightly hold.
Laughter echoed through the grass,
As flowers danced, they formed a mass.

Bees in bow ties buzzed with flair,
Chasing butterflies through the air.
Roses blushed, playing coyly,
While daisies laughed oh-so-joyfully.

Tulips pranced in a funny line,
Waving petals, feeling fine.
Each thorny stem a comedian,
In this vibrant, green coliseum.

As sunlight dipped, the garden glowed,
With punchlines that only blooms bestowed.
What a riot, this floral show,
In nature's jesting undertow!

Garden's Quiet Reverie

In a peaceful plot, where laughter lies,
Where daisies giggle and the rose sighs.
In each petal floats a quirky thought,
A silent joke that time forgot.

Hush, the violets plot and scheme,
Underneath the dusk's soft beam.
Whispering petals tease the dawn,
A fool's parade upon the lawn.

The sunflowers yawn, stretch their necks,
Dreaming loudly, what silly specs!
Gardens filled with gentle glee,
In the quiet, it's plain to see.

Bumblebees in tiny hats,
Buzzing softly like chatty chats.
A lovely space of blooming jest,
In nature's quirky, lively fest.

Blooming Realities and Fantasies

Petals spill tales, as they bloom,
Witty gardens that lift the gloom.
A dandelion dressed like a king,
Makes wishes fly on a giddy wing.

Tulips wear glasses, oh so sleek,
Connoisseurs of the fun they seek.
Each bud a dreamer, wild and free,
Producing laughter, like a jubilee.

Dewdrops twinkle, glisten bright,
Counting stars through the hilarity of night.
Every leaf whispers a joke or two,
In this land where the flowers woo.

As the moon giggles, throws a show,
Each bloom joins in the midnight glow.
A garden grand, a whimsical spree,
Where laughter blossoms endlessly.

www.ingramcontent.com/pod-product-compliance
Lightning Source LLC
Chambersburg PA
CBHW060131230426
43661CB00003B/385